SEARCHING FOR ICARUS

POEMS FOR THE SOUL'S JOURNEY

SEARCHING FOR ICARUS

Poems for the Soul's Journey

SUSAN DAWN

PENNSYLVANIA

Susan Dawn Spiritual Connections, LLC
Lititz, PA
www.susandawnspiritual.com

Library of Congress Control Number: 2025914209
ISBN Paperback: 979-8-9882881-6-9
ISBN Ebook: 979-8-9882881-7-6

Cover Design by Andrew Brown, designforwriters.com
Interior Design by Rebecca Brown, designforwriters.com

Visit the author's website at www.susandawnspiritual.com

Printed in the United States of America

For the love that never stopped calling me home…
You're in every line.

Contents

My son, I caution you to keep
the middle way, for if your pinions dip
too low the waters may impede your flight;
and if they soar too high the sun may scorch them.
Fly midway.

— Ovid, *Metamorphoses*, Book VIII
(trans. Brookes More, 1922)

It was never the fall
that broke us, Icarus,
but forgetting that we
could touch the sun.

— Susan Dawn, *Icarus III*

Listen.

Listen very closely.

I'm going to share
my heart now,
and it's up to you
(not me)
how you hold it
in your hands.

I'm not the girl from yesterday,
or the unfinished echo
of the woman I thought I'd be,
or all the versions in between
that even I have still to meet.

I'm shedding my skin
of myth and memory,
rediscovering my soul
in the art of my becoming
someone new—
someone who is true
to what she kept inside.
And let me be clear—
I'm yet undefined
and no one will characterize
the soul of me but me.

I'm no longer the nice girl
so you'll accept me,
or the sweetheart
so you'll respect me,
or the pleaser
just to keep you
from disappearing
like I never existed
at all.

I exist
but not because you say I do—
not because you look at me
or will someday speak to me
or because we share
some heart-shaped memories.

No, dear World…

I exist
because I AM.
And I bear witness
to myself.

No, I'm not the girl you knew
hidden in the yesteryear,
or the version carried
in the stories we shared

a month or a lifetime ago.
Oh, yes.
I loved her, too.
But she's enfolded into
someone altogether new
and braver, bolder, better
from having burned away
all that was meant to flatter
but instead kept me secret
from myself.

(You don't have to like her.
I've got that covered now.)

Listen.

Listen very closely.

This heart is open
for those who choose to invest
in its precious depths,
to walk the temple path,
and pass through the sacred door
that I've crafted within the crucible
of my own becoming.
I'll only be met by those who
meet me where I stand
unapologetically unafraid

of the thunder or the sun
or what the mirror dares to do

and I would be remiss
if I didn't say,
I wish the same
for you.

Susan Dawn

THE CALL

ICARUS I

The sky beckons,
vast stretches of
everywhere
and nowhere
and everything
at once,
directing his heart
to fly higher
than gravity would allow.

Wings sewn with warning,
he tethered together
fragile prayer
and reckless wonder,
bound by an ethereal thread,
woven by temptation,
and laced with longing,
stitching the space
between logic and lore.

His father warned him—
don't stray,
keep to the middle way—
but how do you ask a flame
to warm and never burn,

to be light,
but never shine?
How do you beg a soul
to listen to reason
when meaning
is fleeting?

Didn't you know, Icarus?

There's more than one way
to reach the sun.

ARROWS

When I was young
I shot a blank arrow—
up, away, gone.
Now I'm older,
bold, brave, and stronger,
chasing arrows into the sun.

THE SKY WAS MADE FOR US

The sky was made for us—
not for the golden finches
who search for sustenance
beneath a broken earth,
feasting at fields
they failed to sow.

Nor the invisible wind
that wanders the while,
directionless,
never knowing the weight
of locked gates
or a gilded cage.

Nor the monotony of stars
who burn a brilliant refrain,
a lingering legacy
light-years away,
names etched in constellations
on the fallen floor—
a walk of shame
instead of the Milky Way.

The sky was made for us—
us, who trace our stories

for the poets and peasants
who script dreams in the air
and seed woven wishes
that never till the ground.

Us, who taste the rain
on the tips of our tongues—
unspoken truths and
calls to rise
that feed the mind,
to flourish and defy
instead of drown.

Us, who search for infinity
in the wild unknown
of supernovas and ancient rivers
led by latent lifetimes of
holy remembrance
that what was ours
was taken
and willed to be returned.

The sky was made for us,
but it never belonged
to any
one
at all.

BRAVERY

The fragile bird looks up,
whispers, "Fear,
I know you're here.
But so is love
and hope and faith.
We can walk this world
together."

ONE AND TWO & ME AND YOU

I want to fly to a place
where time isn't kept—
where we remain blissfully unaware
of the tick-tock
of the infinite clock
so that hours pass
in minutes
and minutes last
for days,
and the heart beats
to its own metronome of
one and two
and me
and you.

LOVE

You looked at me,
and the world stopped—
as if it, too,
held its breath
for what came next.

IT WAS ALWAYS YOU

I knew you before the spark of dawn,
before light birthed the world,
before time unfolded,
before silenced turned to sound

and we ever touched the ground.

I knew you before the first man roamed,
before the rivers ran,
before the flowers bloomed,
before blue skies split open

and the stars exploded.

You're the breath that gives me life
and the blood that bears our sacrifice.
You're the catalyst of my creation,
and the heart of my salvation.

You're the echo in my bones;
the future I've always known
before absence had a name,
before love was my refrain.

Twin Flame.

CHANNEL

Channel this living gift—
this marriage of heart and mind.
Together, they dance in rhythmic transition
and thirst for this blessed life.

THE CANYON AND THE CROSS

In the caverns of my heart I dreamed
that it was you and me
on the edge of a cliff—
this very precipice—
with so much down below
and so far still to go.
A starlit canyon stretched before us
but we knew it couldn't deter us.
Even canyons can be crossed.

We'd hiked for years alone,
always searching on our own,
daylight to our backs,
never crossing paths,
thirsting for all we thought we lacked.
We cried out across these barren lands,
begging for someone to take our hand,
until we heard that still, small whisper—
a blessed redeemer, our holy savior.
We turned our faces to the sun.

The whisper grew stronger—
the rush of a river—
leading us to our salvation,

a reunion in exaltation.
The next words flowed freely:

"Oh, dear children,"
we heard infinite wisdom.
"Follow me now,
down this road to my kingdom.
Within the desert lies your oasis,
my Heaven on Earth, our co-creation—
for while you've thirsted, life has been given.

"This heartbeat of the earth hums everlasting,
and if you listen, you'll hear what I'm asking.
You've never crossed this canyon alone.
Clear your heart; see what you're shown.
Your footprints echo a love that lasts,
but the way is forward, not bound to the past.

"Come, walk this ravine with me.
Come, my children, and you'll see
you were never lost but newly found,
as everything in bloom
once began below ground.
These are the seeds you scattered
centuries ago.
These are the roots you planted
before your soul was known.

"Shake the dust from your battered heart,
shed the cloak of all you think you are.
Go within to that hallowed space,
heed these words and feel my grace:
We are parted only in mind.
I've been with you since the dawn of time."

Darkness gave rise to light
at that canyon's edge,
through the thick of night.
These two heartbeats the only sound,
our echoed song above holy ground—
a sacred tune our souls remembered,
stirring within these ancient embers.

Daybreak on the horizon.
A new beginning has arisen.
This canyon and the cross.

THE CALL

I rest at the threshold
between ferns that bask
in the shade of
green-laced luxury,
beneath the olive tree
that drinks the light
of the sun.
And I, the bridge,
carrying the call
of both.

THE WILLOWS AND THE WINE

Heaven whispers its secrets
among the willows and the wine—
a message for the poet
from the Holy Mother time.
In this garden, on the ground
the sacred petals fall,
a truth revealed, a plea retained
for treasures unrecalled.
Still inside the golden heart
this whisper will be heard,
a prayer embedded with simple grace:
protect the one-winged bird.

GRANDMA

Beauty had a name,
and you answered to it.
Age can't strip away,
as you slip away,
a soul as it bends to light.

I MAY NOT BE A MOTHER

There are no
sweet echoes of giggles
to coax out of frowns
like sunshine parting clouds,
or nightmares to be shushed,
or tears to wipe from rose-red cheeks
after sudden tumbles and silent falls.

There are no
loose teeth placed beneath pillows
in exchange for a fairy's dollar,
or "some assembly required"
toys ready for birthday breakfast
or wrapped from Santa
beneath Christmas tree boughs
boasting homemade ornaments.

There are no
missing socks and mismatched shoes,
or discarded Lego bricks barely used,
or well-hugged dolls and snuggle-me blankets,
or one-of-a-kind art
displayed like a Picasso for the fridge.

There are no
"is this you and me?"
crayon drawings,
or "come and see"
tug of the hand
like a pull on the heartstrings,
or "I love you"
from little voices
that flip my heart around.

I may not be a mother,
but I have been a mother.
I have held tightly
to those who have fallen
and not known how to help
themselves back up,
sat up all night in solidarity,
shooing away monsters in their mind.
I have wiped tears from desperate eyes,
coaxed smiles from stoic faces.
I have been the sunlight
on someone's rain-filled day.

I may not be a mother,
but I have mothered
women with wrinkled hands
and fading memories
who remember old songs

like the children they were yesterday.
"One, two, buckle your shoe…"
There have been meals
for proper nourishment,
tough love talks
in the passenger seats of cars,
"I love you" hugs and "you'll be okay" refrains—
a chorus I will sing until my final day.

I may not be a mother,
but I have been a mother,
to generations of ideas,
birthing creations from seedlings,
from the very core of my being,
watching them mature with the seasons
under the tender care
of my own nurturing hand.
I've sat up at night wondering,
imagining, pondering,
how to bring to fruition
visions years in gestation
that might one day change the world,
or one precious moment,
for one precious someone.

I may not be a mother,
but I have mothered
my own fears

and doubts
and hushed and hugged
my inner child
who constantly wonders
if she is doing enough,
being enough,
loving enough…
I've looked at portraits I've drawn,
the Picasso of my very life,
proclaiming, "this is you and me," dear child.
Your life is your greatest creation.

I may not be a mother.
But I am Mother just the same.

SEEDLINGS

Plant the garden
of influence and endeavor,
buds bearing truth
in timeless measure.
Consecrate in reverence
with radiance and rain,
as lineage lingers
in each sacred name.
Let hands not yet wrinkled
gather the bloom
and carry the essence
from cradle to tomb.

LUKE 17:21

I knelt before my holy altar, prayed,
and heard an ancient voice reply.
It hummed a universal song,
rising from the sacral
like the sacred ascent of dawn:
"Don't forget that virtue is grace
nor forsake the nocturnal order of fate.
Magic weaves the myth
where reason deludes the rhyme
of the sanctity of soul."
I worship within
this hidden realm.

BAPTISM

Summer sculpts
the blessed message,
composes perfect refrains
in its baptismal rains.
Naked, I sketch tracings
of constellations
to pass the time
in this great, grand design.

IS THIS LIFE?

Rain drips from cluttered gutters,
droplets catching blades of tall grass
like early morning dew.
I think: I'll have to mow again tomorrow.
(Is this life?)
Nighttime sets the sun to sleep,
but the yard alights, awakened
by the first fireflies of early June,
blinking into existence
while stars above
exhale their last living breath.
I've never felt so small and insignificant—
a speck of fleeting light wandering
beneath this vast canopy of meaning.
I never dreamed we could matter this much—
lingering for light-years in
heart and mind while Time
strips the bone and breath
and we become
s t a r d u s t .

EARTH

The earth
shakes off the plague of man
while crocuses breach the
broken ground—
dreams take root again.

ASH & BLOOM

Young and naïve, I once believed
in a better world.
Then fantasy turned
and belief was burned,
cloaked in the ash
of threats and regrets.
Heartbeat in my hands,
etched in the bones of the land,
I felt the tenor-tremble of
her holy testament.

So instead I dreamed
of a better world
where rivers ran unbroken
and mountains reigned, a token
to their place among
stars and stone.
But nightmares invaded
where hope once persuaded,
while castles crumbled,
and despair took its throne.

So then I fought
for a better world,
turning scars into armor

so nothing could harm her,
shrouded in darkness
to keep her safe from our sin.
But shadows conspired
where courage once inspired,
and fate stood defiant
 in a war we'd never win.

So I decided to build
a better world.
Seeing through new lenses
and shedding my defenses,
I lay beside the ruins
of reason and riot.
Echoes of the absent,
and flush with the innocent,
she awakens the wild
while faith roots in the quiet.

A new world can be born.

RISE

(R)EVOLUTION

We breathe fire
through crowded streets,
fusing hunger with hope
into cracks of concrete.

We stitch sacred stories
into threadbare seams
and deposit desire
in the banks of our dreams.

We carve our names
into rough drafts of trees
knowing their hidden roots
merge our collective histories.

We are a people held,
trapped by authority.
United, we create
a new world of sovereignty.

RISE

Soften, trust,
let the whole world hold you.

Lean, love,
let the heart echo wide.

Still, listen,
let the truth flow through you.

Breath, rise—
you are here, alive.

LIGHT DOESN'T DECIDE

It isn't wealth that shifts the tide,
nor fate rewoven, realigned.
Not devotion, not a battle cry,
not a script, a map, or grand design.

You came with all you'll ever need—
one purpose, whole, already freed:

To stand unshaken in your soul,
to breathe as light, as love made whole.
Not striving towards a distant spark,
but shining now, dissolving dark.

Light doesn't decide which path to take,
nor bends beneath the shadow's weight.
It simply glows without decree,
just is, just shines, and sets us free.

So be.

(The world is better
because you're in it.)

CHOICE

To be
(or not)
is the arc of your evolution,
the point of your power—
a moment of reckoning
made again and
ad infinitum, beyond,
asking, who do you choose
to be?

IN THE DEEP I BREATHE

I was born for open spaces
where silence sings
a lyrical verse,
and sorrow and wonder
share the same marital bed,
and language strains
to keep up
with the wandering soul.

My complexity
is the key that sets me free.

If you want to find me,
look beneath the shallow,
past the ego's shoal—
the danger zone of your
own self-deception.
I'll be waiting
in the undertow,
where most hold their breath.

In the deep
is the only air I breathe.

RESONANCE

In the hush beyond language,
in the breath before sound,
we're already saying
what's always been known.

MOURNING ANTIQUITY

Humanity walks in ignorance
while the wild has been tamed.
What's done is done, for everyone;
nothing goes unchanged.

You track me from your satellites,
chart stars beyond my seas.
Still, I see much more than you—
you erased the heart of me.

I've sheltered them ten thousand years,
long before your breath was born.
But now, my wild has come undone,
its beauty brambled, torn.

As old as time, I'm Time herself—
we're one with eternity.
I do not yield but gently plead
that you'll leave our wild free.

JOURNEY

Remember gentle faith
creates whole-hearted comfort.
Journey there with prayer.

PAINTING THE ABSTRACT

Tell me,
have you found her yet?

The one you've been seeking
through centuries,
across lifetimes,
in that place where you dream—
nestled between sleep and awake?

Have you found the one
who slipped into the abyss
of your heart
and lives in the chasms
of your psyche?

Don't you see?

I have your painting
from my wall,
peeled like wallpaper
and stashed in my memory box—
the heart a work of art.

I wonder what we'll be
in this abstract of you and me.

LONGING

I long to spill my soul
into your hands—
to press the stars
against your skin
so you might feel
what it is to be lit
from within.

IN THE SACRED HOUR

Pavement glistens
from the early morning rain,
reflections of streetlights
passing puddles on the ground.

5am finds me
driving towards you,
answering a call
inscribed in my soul
from lifetimes ago—
a silent summons
carried across centuries,
etched in the substance
of all that I am.

Memories bore witness
upon a grassy knoll,
where sorrow hung heavier
than the rainclouds
and love bled itself
into the womb of the earth.

We prayed to the pulse
of his living mystery,
hands entwined

like the roots of twin trees
as the holy temple fell
and the sacred template
embedded itself
in our DNA.

I remember you—
here—
with me.

ETERNAL

In my soul
lives an eternal spring
from which I drink
instead of drown.

THERE'S TOO MUCH INSIDE

There's too much inside me—
too much for this skin I'm in,
for these open arms
and idle hands
that want to scatter love across
barren lands
and seed it in the broken places.

I offer the forever of long-stemmed
flowers in my words,
and the delight of ice cream
sprinkled with a smile
and the whimsy of a paper boat
that floats for miles
without the risk of flood.

There's so much inside me—
so much for this mind inclined
to paint the world
in rainbow tiles
and dangle treble clefs
from telephone wires
and tuck handwritten notes
into hidden spaces.

But all I hear is rejection's refrain:
the world isn't ready
for you yet.

Still, I love anyway.

MANTRA

Draw the breath
in its electric power
and chant the rhythm
of this divine supply.

SUNNY DAYS

My cat chases sunbeams
across the kitchen floor,
fractals of light
scattering like fleeting prayers
as he searches for what
won't ever be caught.
Surrendered,
he sprawls across sunspots
until the shadows fall
and sleep calls.

I want to chase the light
across my life
with wild abandon
and rooted trust,
even if I never
hold it long enough
to name it mine.

SOUL

If only we could accept faith
and flow in wisdom and courage,
would we touch the soul?

THE MUSE

Conduct your passive symphony
with tools of your trade
and I'll observe in metaphor.
Sculpt silhouettes subjected to scorn,
predestined to perform,
and I'll play the silence—
a musical monument
where white marble shimmers raw.

Sacred notes chide the flesh
exposing external flaws
of the composer's genius,
forging beauty and forgoing reality.
Angles spin and copper turns,
fleeing translucence and discovering depth
tinged with irony.

Stroke the shoulder of liberty
and indulge in champagne-scented promises
that devour and decay
this woman's wit and wile.

Bare skin charges a static air
as this marble façade canvases

a woman's secret
beneath carved rock and broken curves.

A heart is buried there.

DARK

Dark feminine goddess,
sing a word of secret truth,
transcend your mystery garden
and give life to sun and moon
in this realm of living love.

WHEN WE BUILD CATHEDRALS

She waits in the arch
of a centuries-old cathedral,
concealed beneath a canopy
of wooden rafters and ancient timber,
sitting vigil without story
while hymns and homilies
and the holy cry of sacred hearts
echo in the hallowed hall below.
Her maker carved her
into the high beam,
etching fine lines
along the curve of her wings,
folded forever, at rest,
her fragile beak faintly parted
to share in the chorus of her
four-chambered heart.

I share my heart in silence, too—
carve hope into blog posts
buried in the algorithm,
share stories of grace spoken into
the absence of audience,
channel love through spaces
between silences.
I lay my living legacy

brick by brick, page by page
embedded in the marrow of the world.
This is my cathedral,
chiseled from soul and
stained-glass
and scripture—
truth born from presence,
not pulpits.

But who looks up,
or sees deep beneath?
This open sanctuary
welcomes the weary
finding refuge in its pews,
but there is no altar here—
only a remembered vow
to be a candle in the night.
What meaning will remain
when the carvings are complete
and the scaffolding falls away?
What place do I have
in the history of the heart
when all that I'm building
is invisible to the gilded eye—
a bird with a song

perched in the rafters,
concealed within the cathedral's
bone and beam, hymn unheard
and no less holy.

"No one will see her,"
they goaded with glee.
Her maker molded anyway.
That's not why we create
beautiful things.

THE DESCENT

ICARUS II

What happened
when Icarus fell?
Did he drown beneath
the cerulean sea?
Was his naked body
cradled by its waves,
the weight of his wings,
sodden with wax and water,
keeping him from soaring higher?

Or did he drag himself
to the vacant shores
of his own humility,
crawling on his
hands and knees
in reticence and regret,
a layer of surrender
that can only be known
when you fly

and then fall.

I want to ask him about the before:
How did it feel to soar
so close to the sun—

did you recognize Helios
or did it feel like hell—
that scorching gaze
turned to you
like you were a chosen one.

Did freedom feel free,
following the flock
who have never known
what it means to be caged?
Did you tell them?
Did you whisper
how lucky they were
to have only ever known
wind beneath God-given wings?

Tell me, Icarus,
who you were before
and what became of you
after.

LOST

Map verbs along the Milky Way;
Turn left off the edge of reason.
You won't know you've gone too far
until you're drifting through celestial seasons.

THE STARS DON'T LOOK THE SAME

I searched the stars for years,
making wishes and counting dreams,
but I never saw them, truly,
until I saw you.
Hundreds of winter evenings
chasing sunsets in my car—
down wide-open roads,
music musing,
crooning from the stereo
until the sun-dusted sky
brushed its lips against the
moon-mirrored night
the way you once kissed me.
One ancient summer ago,
we pulled off along the highway—
a secret spot you knew—
and waited for the fireflies,
clusters of light from light-years away
breaching the atmosphere
for us here
in a little alcove on the route.
The stars were always there,
aware, guiding the night
when we held each other

by the fire pit in your backyard,
wordlessly mindful of
the snap and crackle
while we fed the flame.
Every moment was sacred
in the sanctuary of us.
I know you loved me then.
I loved you, too.
I still breathe your name
in the tender pockets of my soul.
The stars don't look
the same without you.

SONG

I wrote my soul
into a song
that you chose
not to sing.

LEFT TO THE RAIN

I was there through the downpour—
when the sun disappeared
behind grey clouds
and the skies broke open
and poured into your heart,
chased by thunderbolts
and lightning strikes
that tried to keep me at bay.
You pushed me away,

but I stayed.

Through wild winds
that tossed debris
and hurled
targeted obscenities,
I sought cover for us,
myself exposed
to the hailstorm that came.
Chilled to the bone,

still I stayed.

But then one autumn day,
when my skies darkened,

you couldn't hold
the umbrella

even when it
simply rained.

SACRIFICE

Sacrifice
   Sacrifice
      Sacrifice…
What will it take
before I think twice?
Releasing the dreams
I used to see
of the love I wanted to be:
Mother. Partner. Lover.
How many times
do I let go,
sacrifice my heart
for the sake of your soul?

Love, please set me free.

LOVE INFINITY

Hush, now.
Quell the fears,
quiet the tears,
and silence the whispers
that threaten defeat,
this hum everlasting,
mocking:
"You're never enough."
Remember love?
It was times infinity,
this song you wrote
upon ancient parchment,
waxing in an Edenic script
that calls for purpose and promises.
Do you remember love?
now it's buried and blurred,
the ink so smudged
it's hard to recall
anything was ever
written there at all.
Remember faith?
Existing in quiet utopian myth,
a waking dream where
innocence lasts
longer than the ever after,

where answers are whispered
under winter skies
without a word spoken.
Hush.
Do you remember faith?
You followed blindly—
a path that spiraled past
the waters where Lethe flattered
and you flirted
and we wept that you
might remember us at all.
Remember hope?
"Perched on the soul,"
do you remember hope at all?
Hush, now...
Hush—
and quiet the tears;
do you hear?
A tune that stirs the soul,
and shepherds the lost,
and wakens the listless,
this hum everlasting,
singing...

Remember me?

SEPARATION

Circle the spirit
that wills itself to logic,
measuring the dawn of love
like the last living light.

IF I COULD ASK YOU
ONE THING

My life has existed
in the space between goodbyes,
and I'm not ready
to say another—
not while the dandelion tea
is still warm in my mug,
and my dog still nuzzles her head
in the crook of my neck,
and the Canasta cards
are still being dealt—
one red three for you,
and one wild card for me.

I've held enough endings
in the curve of these hands,
seen enough names carved in stone—
Beloved One, Rest in Peace
to all the souls I loved
and the selves I outgrew
and the house at the front of the street
that was my hearth of healing
and the heart of my
once upon a dream.

Love lives on in sacred memory,
but grief gathers in hidden corners
like avoided cobwebs on the ceiling,
and fear lingers beneath the threshold
of every new hello,
looming at the edge of the frame
of each picture-perfect moment of
unmediated joy.

I just want you to stay
for a little while longer.
Maybe forever,
if you can.

ATRIUM

Don't let these long days
make you grow cold.
Don't let the bitterness seep
into the atrium of your heart—
glass castles clouded by rain
when all along they were windows
to the soul, meant to let in
the sun.

THE TREES OR ME

I wonder if trees cry
at the first hint of autumn.
I wonder if they sense
pigment fading
from their leaves,
if they sigh, resigned,
a song of surrender
knowing resistance
would only prolong
the pain of inevitable change.
I wonder if they inhale sharply
when the first leaf releases—
f l o a t i n g,
    f l o a t i n g,
        f l o a t i n g
to rest in peace
with the earth.
I wonder if they turn
to their brothers and sisters
standing for decades beside them,
see canopies tinged
fire and gold,
and offer care and comfort:
"It's okay. See?
It's happening to me, too."

I wonder if they try
in vain to hold on,
even as November's wind
blusters until it's breathless
and then tries, tries again
to shake loose the memory
of the past,
the very foundation
they cling to,
in order to be birthed again.
I wonder if they beg
for more time,
as if Time means anything
to the ancient ones—
one more day (they pray)
before they're left
vulnerable
and barren
and disarmed.
I wonder.

TREE

The tree breathes out.
I breathe in.
What an intimate
exchange of life.

LOVE IS NEVER WASTED

Grief is the living presence—
it betrays the breath,
etches scars on evanescent hearts,
burrows into the bones, unbidden,
like a temporal ache
on grey-skied days.

It curls beneath the ribs
that once brought life
and tucks itself into
the corners of Time,
weaving through
golden-hued memories
of all the yearnings left behind.

I woke with the dawn,
the ticking clock echoing
numbers of angels
dancing in stunning synchronicity
while she exhaled
the last breath
from her lungs.

Tears and laughter
mingle and merge

with memory—
the epitome of a life
well-loved.

Strange,
what the heart can hold—
how much ache and awe
we are.

I've touched beyond the veil
but empty chairs
and absent rings
trigger the mourning
and the missing.

Being human is messy magic
when you live
the paradox of feeling,
and grief becomes the shadow
of a once-existed love.

3AM

Ghost thoughts
and unhealed shadows
clamor for attention,
emerging from the caverns
in which you hid them.
Nothing good happens
at 3am.

I PRAY WHEN NO ONE'S LISTENING

Idealism is stripped bare,
naked,
surrendered to the sacrifice
of this half-life we lead
for lack of resources
and too much of everything else.
"Pray to me," you whisper
in this early morning refuge
before the sun burns the horizon
and ghosts in the dark
flee on the breeze.
"Come, lay your troubles
at my altar,
where I may guide and comfort
if you only surrender."
Letting go
down the rabbit hole—
gravity pulls in everything
and nothing
and on
　　and on
　　　　and on
　　　　　　you fall,
grasping for a hollow reprieve.

Surrender doesn't matter
when no one's left
to take up arms.
"Come in from the cold," you say.
I step into the fire.
A beating, bleeding heart
burns with a thousand
unanswered prayers
where silence is still
and faith trembles from the effort.
Illusions stir, turn to ash
while youth decays—
folly to think it could be
captured, caged
in a thought, a bottle,
a wish like this.
Incinerate, disintegrate—
there is no phoenix here.
(God)
How broken do you have to be
before you hear the *we* in me?

THE DESCENT

Words are all that remain
within a weary heart
whose voice is rugged, raw,
choking obscenities
and vomiting stolen dreams,
crying for a savior when
abandonment reigns supreme.

DARKNESS BEFORE DAWN

Pain will bring you to your knees.
(So fall to your knees.)
Pain will make you cry in grief.
(So cry and cry some more.)
Pain will make you question
everything
and everyone
and yourself
until there's nothing left
but what's held here within.
Pain will deceive you,
claim you as weak.
(Remember that you're strong.)
This is the darkness before the dawn.

ASK

As I lay me down to sleep…
I stare at the cracks in my ceiling,
willing your form to seep
through as some holy message,
a miracle made for me.
I pray thee, Lord, my soul to keep.
You send roses from the sky
and marble statues who weep.
Where is my miracle?
Where is my peace.

REVIVE THE HEART

Dear God,
Help me.
Cauterize this
open wound
that leaks longing
where there's latency;
and revive the heart
that flatlined
from the ghosted fantasy;
and sew and bind
the place inside
that seeks more
than this faulty prophecy.

Dear God,
please offer me
this remedy.

I beg and plead,
fix these fractured
parts of me,
where the dark night
spins and spirals
in this chronic tragedy.
I sleep to wake

and wake to dream,
pulled down by
aching gravity
and crawl to hope
and reach for faith
and find scars and stars
in somatic symmetry.

Dear God,
heal me.
Don't let this be
my legacy.

"Dear child,"
the words rise like memory.
"You were never broken."

Rebirth

YOU ARE HERE

When you carry the world
on those tired shoulders,
remember you are here.
When your reflection reveals
what you believe you lack,
remember you are here.
When your mind shouts obscenities,
burdened by your memories,
remember you are here.
When your pain tries to steal your breath,
and your heart burns with every regret,
remember you are here.
You are here, and not by accident.
You are here, your heart still innocent.
You are here, part of the pulse of the world.
You are here, a gift of the soul.
You are here.
You are here.
You are here.
Stay.

HEAL

Some mending of a life
transforms the weary into light.
Heal me here as above.

I SENSE THE RAIN

I stumble up cracked concrete steps
to a brownstone caught
in shadow,
follow you into the house
where cobwebs drape from curtains
and dust scatters beneath our feet.

On the floor by the staircase
lies a single sock,
shredded heel-to-toe,
and a birch broom stands in the corner,
splintering at the grip.

There's a dip in the couch cushions,
empty water glasses on the table.
Faded pictures line the mantle,
though the shades are drawn.

"I know this place," I whisper.
"But it's been so long…"
I sense the rain within me.
"Can we stay?" I pray.

You pause, hand me the broom
to clear the cobwebs away.
"I never left," you say.

ANCESTOR

Ancestor, cleanse this karma deep.
Merge holy bud and sacred tree
beneath winter sky and summer sea;
perform this perfect offering.

WARRIOR REFLECTED

It rushes back in memory,
leaving me breathless—
how I stayed,
what I survived.
Pain turned to purpose,
purpose became passion,
and in every moment,
I willed myself on.

Evolution happens in stages.
Maybe healing does, too.
Strength and fire,
I see it all so clearly
when I turn around
and look behind me—
where I've been
to get to here I am.

She is who I used to be,
so much younger,
begging for miracles,
crawling her way home
to hope.
She learned to be held,
carried and cradled—

the warrior
in the mirror
now.

BURN

Show me the flames.
Engulf me in fire.
Watch me burn.
Let me love.

I, THE FLAME

I was your golden glow
painting the earth
in the moment before
the sun knew sky;
the breath in your lungs
when words choked
and silence tasted like bitterroot;
the hand unseen
pressing stars into your chest
so you wouldn't forget
you were made of them.

I was the ground beneath your exile—
the barefoot prayer
that carried your name
in the safety of my cells.

You called it dangerous—
the way I loved.
But it was only your shadow
shielding itself from truth.

You reached for softness,
but your hands were calloused
from all the burdens you bore,

and I picked up each cross
as my own weight to carry—
splinters in the faded scars
on my heart.

I know I was never yours
to keep or tame—
like a river rushes onward,
so do you.

But you live in the spaces
of my sentences,
and I live in the closed chapters
of your heart—

the fire and the flame,
we were always meant
to show each other
the way.

ROOTS

Roots grow in the dark,
tangled masses a mess
of contradiction—
burrow downwards
just to break through
and meet the sun.

THE FORGET-ME-NOT

Today I found myself
in the garden we'd planted
in the seven-year cycle
of our early union's bloom.
I followed the familiar path
to its center—
skipped the stones overrun with moss
and ambled through the rusted gate
that sings when it swings open.
The brick wall that keeps its secrets
is thick with brittle ivy—
a reminder that everything
decays with time
and, maybe, so did we.
Do you remember
when we planted the two lemon trees?
The sour memory of isolation
after so many summers
spent every day together—
just add a pinch of sugar,
I'd beg. Just see me, meet me
here in the garden again.
But you'd close the gate
and go away
and wouldn't let me in.

We didn't expect the cardamom
growing wild between words—
stolen glances,
sweet heat in the silence.
We dug in the dirt, down into the depths,
unwrapping the scent
spiced with ancient memory.
You awakened the woman in me.
We sprinkled seeds
with wild abandon, trusting
what would bloom.
We planted red roses. You called them yellow.
I guess we never had a chance at all.
Oh, but this is still
my sacred place, you know.
It's the sanctuary inside me,
and though the lemons spoiled,
and the cardamom crushed,
and the flowers withered
from too long in thirst,
this garden will always be ours.
Still—
I tend the forget-me-not
of roots revived
in second chances
blooming, renewed,
at the heart of it all.

HEART

The heart loves
(it beats)
it breaks
(it beats)
on and on and on.

I WANT WHAT'S REAL

I want what's authentic—
what you're sheltering beneath
the mask you so carefully crafted
that even you don't realize
you've been wearing all along.
I want to see what's inside
the secret corners of your mind
and the chambers of your heart
you've kept equally caged,
collecting scars
and covered cobwebs
from a lifetime of neglect.
I know it scares you.
I've been there, too,
hiding behind a door
fastened with a thousand locks.
But don't you know?
This lover is the locksmith,
but I only hold one key,
and if you'd look deep enough,
you'd see you're holding one, too,
with the same grooves
and curves
and crevices
that unlocks the heart of me

wanting to open up to you.
So tell me...
tell me everything you feel,
tell me everything that's real.
Tell me with an honesty
that makes you shiver and
surrender on your knees.
I'll be here,
in surrender beside you.
I want what's true.
I want you to hand me your heart
not knowing what I'll do.
I'll surprise you, treasure it—
I'll put it in my chest
so you are never alone,
and we'll set the fears to rest.
I'll take my own heart
and place it in your hands
as the symbol of trust
we both need.

BELOVED

To love is to place your heart
in the hands of your beloved,
an intimate prayer:
"Keep this safe for me."
And the beloved will.

LIKE WATER INTO WINE

True beauty
exists in your rawness,
in the vulnerability
of your sovereign truth.
So, show off the scars,
your hidden battle wounds.
Tell me what you've been through.
I want to know
what you survived.
Share with me your
secrets and shame,
and I'll show you mine,
and let's love them all away
inside the vault of the heart,
alchemizing pain into triumph
like water into wine.

ALCHEMY

Transcend the myth
that separated spirit
and kept us bound to ego.
Diamonds are forged in fire,
but we became the flame.

BORN OF THE FIRE

The hum of the television
and age-old conversations
droned on behind me,
but I, all of five,
would sit by the hearth
and let my cheeks grow
rosy-warm by the glow
of the fireplace light.
I'd watch the orange hue
flicker and fall
to its own scattered rhythm—
a subtle song in the snap
and crack from dry-dusted logs.
The world around me faded
and in the imagined places
grew a story of a fiery realm
and the princess who lived there,
trapped by the cinder.
For years, she waited, perched
on the highest log,
dodging heat and memory
and idly watching everything
turn thick with smoke and ash,
wondering if the same
would ever become of her.

Then one day,
feeling reckless and brave,
she stepped too close.
The flames nipped at
her slippers and tinged
the hem of her gown,
but instead of running away,
she reached down,
held the frayed fabric
in her soot-coated hands.
In that moment, she knew
she never had to be afraid.
She was born of the fire,
and the fire she became.

RESURRECTION

Words create wounds,
crawling through catacombs
and poisoning the well
of a once-holy heart.
Oh, forgiveness, find me here,
in this resurrection of the sacred.

LIKE THE PHOENIX YOU ARE

Let the fire burn you.
Let it consume you.
Let all of your anger
point to your pain.
Let it ignite a primordial blaze,
heat you up from the inside out,
turning everything you
thought you were
to ash.
Rage on
and on and
on
and then,
let it soften you,
transform you
to rise
like the phoenix
you are.

REBIRTH

No one tells you
how being born
also feels like dying—
clamor and crawling
through the dark
because you've been
too afraid of flying.

STILL, WE'LL RISE

You feel tired, worn, defeated;
you feel broken, buried done.
You feel bruised, betrayed, and cheated;
you feel all hope is gone.
Well, let me tell you something, love,
let me share a truth—
you've always had the strength you need.
You see, it's part of you.
You can stay in stagnant waters,
you can hold onto all your pain,
but if you grip the past too tightly,
you'll lose more than you'll gain.
So open up the heart now.
Free that shadowed mind.
Here, takes my hand,
I'll show you how
to fall and then to rise.

THE BECOMING

ICARUS III

Do you still curse the sun
when it was the one
that offered warmth
and lit the way,
or grieve the wings
that failed you, claimed
beneath the waves?

Oh, Icarus.
Those wings were never
made for permanence,
but in your solemn ignorance
you lost the way
into the heart of you,
the very start of you.

Burned was the belief
you had to fly higher
to be found—
a feathered crown
of humility, instead
of the glory
you felt bound to be.

Oh, Icarus—
We held you in

silent reverence.
It wasn't the height
that made you holy
or the flight that set you free.
We've tasted the sky, too,
were baptized in the sea.
We hung our hopes on
broken wings, the salt sting
of truth filling our lungs
and the flame the hymn
we'd one day become.

You see...

It was never the fall
that broke us, Icarus,
but forgetting that we
could touch the sun.

WINGS

Anchor deep the will of self,
shimmering with power—
a quiet flight on gossamer wings.

BAREFOOT IN BEGINNINGS

There was a moment—
I don't know when—
the wind felt different on my skin,
and the sky stretched wider,
like it could last forever,
and the birds in the canopies
carried secrets in their song
that matched the hum
beneath my ribs.

Maybe it was the way the sunlight
held to the horizon—
a moment's pause before the dusk—
or the way the river never asked
which way it was going,
just kept flowing
to the tune of its own internal tempo,
trusting the call of the evermore.

Maybe it was the way
my name sounded
when I spoke it out loud—
something I could be proud of,
and how it felt like mine again—
settled into the bridge of my throat

as if I remembered how to come home
and belong to myself.

I don't know when I began again.
I only know I'm here—
bared feet in the dirt,
walking steady on the earth,
ready for what happens next.

BELIEVE

Through chaos and conflict,
despite destruction and division,
between pressure and pain
breathes, still, a beautiful world.

THE ECHO OR THE SONG

I used to be the girl
who waited by closed doors
and hid behind winter coats
in the cubby of a classroom.
I lingered along muted walls
and tiptoed into hidden worlds,
within and beyond the pages of books
and stories where I held the pen,
wanting to feel safe again
at home in this dismal place—
where colors clashed too loudly,
and the rules too hard to follow,
and no one seemed to speak
the language of my soul.
I just wanted to live
where the sacred is.
Now a woman grown,
I sit beside that little girl—
braid wildflowers in her hair,
draw Andromeda in the air.
I remind her that she's always home
as we walk, hand-in-hand,
connected to the earth again.
Believing it's safe to be seen,
I urge her to write the poetry

still imprinted on her earnest heart.
It took a lifetime
to become the one
she always needed me to be,
to reconcile and reawaken
those hidden parts of me.
I'm the echo that became the song.
We're not the shadow anymore.

TRANSCEND

Transcend the past our histories wove
and renew the path your shadow chose;
love returns what Time once stole—
meet me in the sycamore grove.

WHERE YOU UNDRESSED ME

Dozens of moments stand out in my mind—
memories of us frozen in time,
yet so many more seem to be fading
like they never happened at all.
I recall the way you looked at me
when I turned to leave—
your eyes said everything,
and just before I turned the corner,
I looked back over my shoulder
and still, you were standing there.
You crossed the space between us,
called me beautiful beneath your breath
as you held me; I inhaled gently,
breathing in the feel of you.
Where is that man I knew?
I wish I'd met you now instead of then
so we could go back, begin again.
Those hours in the rainstorm,
windshield wipers clearing fog
while we parked along the sidewalk
and talked and talked some more…
So much of my heart is made up of you—
how we almost made it
if only we could have sustained it.
You reached into my soul, rearranged it

so now I'm someone new.
I keep thinking about how you said
you're always thinking of me—
a thousand times in a thousand ways—
and all the days I spent wishing
I had believed you;
you were telling me the truth.
You were the home I found, you know,
before I came home to myself.
And now wherever it is I go,
I go as someone else.
It's the little moments I keep sacred,
secretly locked in my heart,
like the hours-long conversations
or the comfortable silences
and in between, the music.
Oh, the irony of love like this—
you had to become a stranger
so I'm not a stranger to myself.

MERGE

You touch me like scripture;
I answer in prayer.
We align, a holy shrine.

REUNION OF SOULS

Out of the rubble
of your own flawed foundation
you'll crawl,
and I'll be there,
waiting where you
left your soul.

You'll mouth my name
like a vow
you never meant to forget,
and I'll hear the honesty
in your breath
that once was laden with regret.

We'll share tender touches
and lasting looks
and then,
when the silence passes,
we'll speak of what we found
in the wilderness between us—
how I became whole
and you set yourself free.

You'll reach for me,
and I won't brace for goodbye.

I'll reach for you,
and you won't turn away.

Of the many roads we walked
(alone)
they all led back to us.

UNION

He's the light
that called you home.
You're the flame
that lit the way.
Sacred love.

RE-EMERGENCE OF ME

Let me be clear:
I'm not who I used to be.
The version you knew
at thirty-three,
or thirteen,
and every age in between,
has merged with a woman
I'm honored to meet.

She no longer says yes
when she means to say no,
or stays when her heart
implores her to go.
She won't be quiet, compliant,
or bow to the world's whims;
she no longer dilutes herself
for an old, distorted lens.

I've discovered myself,
and I've set my soul free.
You may want something different,
but I've outgrown what you seek.

So keep that same version
in your head if you wish—
I love who I am now,
and I'm better as this.

RENAISSANCE

Make noble the pursuit of happiness
and attune this heart in synthesis—
the renaissance of your desire,
awakened soul of holy fire.

CALL OF THE WILD FEMININE

I've birthed within me
the call of the wild.
Here I am.
Taking up space
with a feral voice,
defending the divine honor
of everything I hold dear.
Fearlessly focused
on the sacred within the soul
I've only just begun
to recognize and recover.
I lit the fire within me,
and I will not relent—
born there in the crucible
of my own becoming,
I crawled on the broken glass
of my once-shattered heart,
made my way through the dark.
I picked up each stray morsel
of fallen ash
to piece myself back together,
reignited within the embers
of those fragmented pieces of me.
I've earned everything I've become.
So do not mistake me

for the silent, simple, or shallow.
I'm none of these.
No longer betraying
the beating of my heart.
No longer abandoning
the avenue of my truth.
No longer doing disservice
to the depths of my divinity—
or yours.
Not for your pleasure,
or the world's comfort.
I walk this earth
with the wild within me,
and I am
unafraid.

DAWN

Holy dawn
and electric night
whisper the infinite song
of sacred light.

DEAR WORLD

You don't know me
as I know myself.
I've explored the depths of my being,
tread through the underworld,
waded through grief
and pain
and tick-tricked trauma
and died and was reborn
over and
over
again.

I've lain with my shadows,
rejoiced in my light,
became one with the no-thing,
before remembering
I'm part of everything.

I've shifted the way I think,
the way I see the world,
and how I view myself,
accounting for every aspect
of my own to the core—

(every fault and flaw
and failure)

while finding in
each hidden corner
the confidence
and belief
and timeless trust—
now without validation
or the approval
of your external reach.

And still there's more.

I became a bitch
to those who cling
to co-dependencies
and betray boundaries
as I healed
my people-pleasing
tendencies.
Yet I am kindness
and compassion
and peace

to those who can see
beyond their own shadow.

I don't mind it.
You are what you think of me.
I am who I know myself to be.

These two truths can co-exist.

I spent a lifetime
in my own process
of becoming
to reach this place.

Here,
where I finally recognize
and embrace
my own sacredness.

Here,
where I walk the earth,
worship her heartbeat
beneath my feet.

Here,
in the middle way
of all I was
and all I will someday be.

Call me what you will.
Judge me as you are.
Reject me if you must.

I love you as I always have.

THE BECOMING

She wove her dreams
with the thread of constellations,
embroidered stars—one by one—
on the quilt of her becoming.

POEM FOR THE
DIVINE FEMININE

She's the combined goddess
of the compassionate warrior
housed within the temple
of everything I was,
everything I am,
everything
I'm about to become.

(Fierce. Formidable.
Tender. True.)

I've traveled lifetimes
to recognize myself
as I do now—
diving into the ancient
catacombs of my heart,
navigating the universal
pathways of my soul,
dying a thousand times
in a thousand moments
to come alive again
and again
and again.

(Reborn,
my feminine rises.)

I've sacrificed myself
to the world—
stifling my voice,
suppressing all emotions,
hiding from my eternal light.

(No more,
I shatter the silence.)

The world pushes back,
shouting outraged contradictions:
"You're not enough!"
"You're too much!"
"Be more!"
"Become less!"

It chips away at me,
creates cratered scars
where love is meant to mend,
not bleed.

(Who did you want me to be?)

I cut these strings
and dive into the core

of my faithful truth,
swimming
through the wild unknown
to claim pieces
of my neglected self,
getting lost and found
and still here I am.

(Here I still am.)

The world tries to smother
the holy flame.
Don't you know
I'm a phoenix
and the embers
are my domain?

Brought to my knees
through a thousand surrenders
I grow stronger
and softer
all at once.

(This is my gift,
my humble offering.)

I'm setting fire to the lies
of all I've been told

and breaking loose
from the shackles
of my existence.

(In this space,
I am the beloved.
In this place,
I am part of the sacred.)

I'm ready to dance
in the wilderness
of all that I am.

(In this moment
I become.)

I set my feminine free.

PHOENIX

They tried to burn you down.
They didn't know
you were the fire.

I AM (NOT) THE GODDESS

I'm not the goddess you knew.
The one that existed
on Mount Olympus
has long been extinguished.
You made sure of that.
So I watched your world burn
in the fires of Pompeii,
lighting my cigarette
in the dying embers of Vesuvius.
I stepped aside,
let the lava cascade,
flicked the remains
towards the screams
and rose like a phoenix
from the ashes
of what you thought you buried.
I saved you all.
Yes, I'm that kind of goddess.
I carried you home,
yet you failed to believe;
you tore down my temples,
cursed at my altar—
begged, cried, no matter—
I heard it all.
Still, I rose from my gilded seat—

the one you painted for me,
and climbed down my pedestal—
the one you sculpted to me,
and held you safe.
Oh, you and your human race.
I am not the goddess you crave,
someone to betray
your sacrifice
and inspire
and answer
your thousand questions
with a thousand stories
and a thousand wordless prayers.
I am so much more
and so much less
than what I seem—
an angel in a sunbeam,
a sprite beholden
to the dark of night.
I am all. I am none.
I am the virgin painted
on the cathedral wall,
the whore condemned
upon the fall.
I am a lifetime of laughter,

seconds of sorrow.
I am profane and vulnerable,
sacred and hallowed.
You, who have forgotten me,
buried me beneath your reality TV,
abandoned me for your social idols,
living in your self-denial...
You toast to me
drinking from your broken cup,
catching a glimpse of me at sun-up,
before the reflection fades,
before the truth is swayed.
Still I stay.
Because I am not the goddess
you thought you knew.
You see, I am also you.

BOOKS BY SUSAN DAWN

Daybreak: Daily Messages to Illuminate Your Spiritual Life
Get guidance when you need it most with motivational messages that illuminate your soul growth journey! Channeled with warmth, love, and compassion, each message in *Daybreak* provides a prompt for conscious reflection to connect you deeper with yourself and help you navigate your spiritual life.

The Unity Code: Rewriting the Twin Flame Template for Your Sacred Union Path of Ascension
Journey into the heart of sacred relationships where love becomes the catalyst for your soul's evolution! Discover a new paradigm of twin flames, soul connections, and divine partnership through remembrance, healing, and embodiment. You are the living energy of love. You are the embodiment of unity consciousness.

You are The Unity Code.

OTHER WRITINGS

The Mystic and the Muse
The Mystic and the Muse is where the mystical meets
the writer's path, where transformation unfolds both
on the page and in life, and where spirituality and
artistry join together to honor the beauty of both the
sacred and the ordinary. Whether through spiritual
teachings, personal essays, or creative musings, this
space is an invitation to journey inward, embrace
transformation, and find meaning in the stories we
live and the ones we create.

Read more at www.themysticandthemuse.info

NOVELS
by Susan Pogorzelski

Gold in the Days of Summer
The Last Letter
Lilac in Winter
East of Everywhere
Ashes in Autumn

FOR YOUR JOURNEY

From healing resources to inclusive learning tools,
continue your soul growth journey by exploring all of
the services and products at
Susan Dawn Spiritual Connections!

The Unity Code Intensive
Higher-Heart Academy
Ascension Connections Portal
(meditations, masterclasses, resource library, and more)
Healing & Harmony Activation Series
Tarot in Translation Series
Spiritual Guides & Journals
Tarot & Oracle Decks

ABOUT SUSAN DAWN

Susan Dawn is an author, holistic spiritual mentor, and energy practitioner at *Susan Dawn Spiritual Connections* with a focus on soul connections, conscious relationships, and the ascension journey. As a natural psychic intuitive, she serves as an intermediary to bring through guidance messages and healing activations for union with yourself, others, and the Universe by nurturing your personal empowerment and encouraging connection to your sacred creativity and authentic magic.

Connect with Susan on social media at @susandawnspiritual!

ABOUT SUSAN DAWN SPIRITUAL CONNECTIONS

Susan Dawn Spiritual Connections is a sacred space for your soul growth journey and the home of the Higher-Heart Academy, Ascension Connections, and Tarot in Translation! Bridging spiritual understanding with real, human application, *Susan Dawn Spiritual Connections* offers everything you need for your soul's expansion and to connect to your divinity within.

Learn more at www.susandawnspiritual.com

ACKNOWLEDGEMENTS

THIS BOOK HAS BEEN A labor of love over twenty years in the making. These poems were written across the seasons of my spiritual journey, each one a reflection of who I was, what I was healing and remembering, and who I was becoming.

It took three frustratingly-long years to compile them into the narrative you now hold in your hands, with the myth of Icarus serving as a symbol for our collective ascension. In writing (or rewriting) each poem, I revisited the landscape of my own becoming—trusting the path that led me here and the soul-voice inside that longed to be shared.

Searching for Icarus is a living testament to not only what I've walked through myself, but also the journey we've found ourselves on together.

Endless thanks to you, reader and friend, for letting me share a piece of my own soul story with you—from the darkest nights to the return home to myself, and everything in between.

To those who have been part of this sacred journey—thank you. Whether you witnessed my path from afar, supported me in silence, or held space through your presence, your energy is woven into these pages. I'm grateful beyond words.

May these words carry the echoes of the rise and fall and (r)evolution within us all.